It's a GAS!

The Allure of the Gas Station

gestalten

Gas Station
MEMORIES
JAY LENO

As a kid growing up in New York and later in New England in the 1950s, visiting a gas station was an adventure. Station attendants (called 'Grease Monkeys' behind their backs) still wore corporate uniforms, usually jumpsuits with matching caps, with the company logo on their backs. My favorite was the big red Texaco star, and the only way they got away with that in the 'Red Scare' McCarthy era was because they were from Texas, and there were no Communists in Texas – that was unimaginable. Gas stations were immaculate in the 1950s, but how could they afford to keep them so clean when gas was only a nickel a gallon?

I remember sitting in the back seat of my parents' 1949 Plymouth, which was enormous. There were no child safety seats back then, or even seat belts, so it was easy to slide over to watch the action while the Grease Monkeys went to work; cleaning the windows, checking the oil and water and tire pressure. Today, only windows need attention, as everything else on a car is self-contained, and 'full service' sounds vaguely sexual anyway to our corrupted 21st-Century ears. The 1950s was a more innocent time, or maybe I was just young and didn't get the innuendo.

Every once in a while we'd pass an extraordinary gas station, designed by some architect who was between real jobs. There were plenty of 'theme' diners and restaurants in New Rochelle, so a futuristic gas station wasn't totally out of context, and they did bring customers in, who must have been curious if pumping gas in some sheet-metal architectural fantasy was any different than the corner station. Of course it wasn't, but I still loved that some stations matched the extravagance of cars at the time, with their

2

canopies spreading like wings, just like the fins on a late '50s Cadillac.

As a kid, a gas station was also one of the only places I could stare at cars without being dragged away by my arm to the store or grandma's house. It was probably the place that planted the seed for my obsession with cars and motorcycles, because you never know what or who you'd see at the station. The advertising men ('Mad Men'!) who commuted into New York had new cars they'd drive on the weekends with their wives, and that's when you'd get to see under the hood of a Cadillac, or even a Corvette if you were lucky. I was as fascinated as every other kid was with new cars, especially rare ones like MGs and Triumphs, as their drivers tried desperately to keep their oil pressure up and their British motors from boiling over in a hot New York summer.

By the 1960s we started to see super-special gas stations in magazines like LIFE and LOOK, and they always seemed to be out in California, and designed by somebody like Richard Neutra. I imagined all gas stations were special out West, where it was always sunny and women drove Thunderbird convertibles or Austin-Healeys while wearing white gloves, and wannabe movie stars and models filled your gas tank. There are still plenty of aspiring actors working mundane jobs in LA, but the Neutra gas stations are gone, and the white gloves.

But gas stations are still a place to check out cars, especially on the weekends in LA, when folks bring out their special rides for a cruise in town, and you never know what you'll see. The gas station is a democratic space, where, like death and taxes, everybody has to go sometime. You'll see a new Bentley in the same station as a beat-up Ford wagon, but only if the Ford is visiting a nice neighborhood! It's also a great place to talk to people about their cars – how do you like it? Is it a piece of junk? What gas mileage do you get? I get asked a lot of questions about the cars I drive when I'm at LA's gas stations. It's the democracy of the fill-up; people get to ask questions, and get to take selfies, and I'm OK with that. I was the curious kid once, in the back seat of my parents' car, hoping to see something or someone interesting during a drive, and especially at a gas stop. How could I say no?

The gas station culture collected in 'It's a Gas!' is remarkable, and opens my eyes to how things were done in other countries. I even learned something about American culture, and how many interesting architects and designers had a hand in creating the coolest stations from the 1920s through today. For instance, I never knew Frank Lloyd Wright designed a gas station for Buffalo in 1927! It was never constructed, which is probably best, as there was a fireplace in the office! There's a photo in this book of the Buffalo Transportation Museum mockup of Wright's station, with glass Art Deco gas tanks hanging from the ceiling.

Enjoy the book! Gestalten does a great job with design publishing, from micro-houses to collector cars and even choppers. 'It's a Gas!' is the best book I've ever seen on gas stations...and the only one! But it's still a great read.

The GAS STATION is *BORN*

Early on, gas stations were rudimentary—
this was uncharted territory, after all.
It's as if oil companies themselves were
oblivious to the dawning of a new age.

The Gas Station Is Born

The world's first gas station was located in Wiesloch, Germany, and was actually a pharmacy. In 1888, Bertha Benz—an automotive pioneer and wife of automobile inventor Karl Benz—stopped to buy petroleum spirits here in order to continue her journey to Pforzheim.

Today, a monument commemorates this historic act of refueling. A few years later, around the turn of the century, cars started becoming widespread in Germany. This created a growing need for places to buy gas. At the time, gas was primarily sold in drugstores, though

hotels and guesthouses also offered it. The first gas stations built in the style we recognize today were found in the U.S., complete with gas pump, a glazed cashier's booth, a roof that shielded rain, and a tall sign visible from afar display prices. In America, the Ford Model T had become so successful that the number of motorists was rapidly on the rise. In the early 1920s, the modern gas station arrived in Europe. Germany's first "real" gas station was established in 1922 on Raschplatz, a square in the city of Hanover. \

Functionality was key. With few drivers on the roads, a pit stop and a couple pumps were the only necessities—an illuminated sign, perhaps. The architecture was secondary and simply mirrored the vernacular.

MOTOR UND SPORT

AUTO GARAGE

The Gas Station Is Born

Odd as it may seem now, buying ...from drugstores and out of the ...le was perfectly normal for ...ers in the early twentieth century. ...ilar gas station concepts live on ...ay in Asia, where glass bottles are ...commonly used as gas canisters.

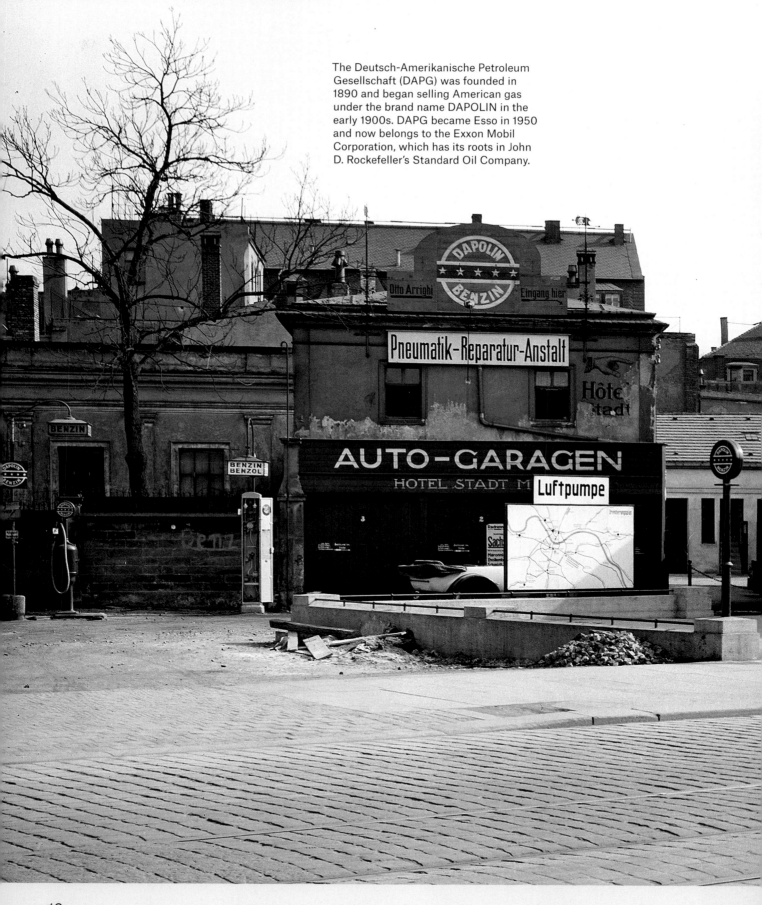

The Deutsch-Amerikanische Petroleum Gesellschaft (DAPG) was founded in 1890 and began selling American gas under the brand name DAPOLIN in the early 1900s. DAPG became Esso in 1950 and now belongs to the Exxon Mobil Corporation, which has its roots in John D. Rockefeller's Standard Oil Company.

In 1945, French photojournalist Paul Almásy took this picture of a gas station in Paris just after the city was liberated. The name suggests a link with Elf Aquitaine, but the former French oil company was not actually founded until the mid-1960s.

There is no way a gas station with a highly flammable thatched roof would get the green light today. This Shell gas station in England was built in the style of a country house a century ago—at a time when fire safety regulations were a little more lax.

Frank Lloyd Wright, perhaps America's most famous architect, designed a gas station to be built in the city of Buffalo, NY in 1927. It was never built, but a decision was made in 2002 to rectify this. Now visitors can admire his work at the Buffalo Transportation Pierce Arrow Museum.

THE 1927
FILLING S[T]
FRANK LL[OYD]
WRIGHT

18

This picture from 1946 shows Germany's condition after the Second World War. In the background you can see one of the many bombed houses. Motor vehicles, such as those seen here refueling at an Esso gas station, would play an essential role in the reconstruction of the country in the second half of the twentieth century.

LEUNA
Feuergefahrlich!
Rauchen.
Hantieren mit offenem Licht
in 5 m Umgebung
polizeilich verboten.
43
BENZIN

Appearing distinctly dated today, this eccentric-looking gas station in Hampshire, England, would have been "de rigeur" in its day. The thatched roofs and leaded windows reflect the craze for mock Tudor, cottage-style architecture that swept through rural Britain in the 1930s.

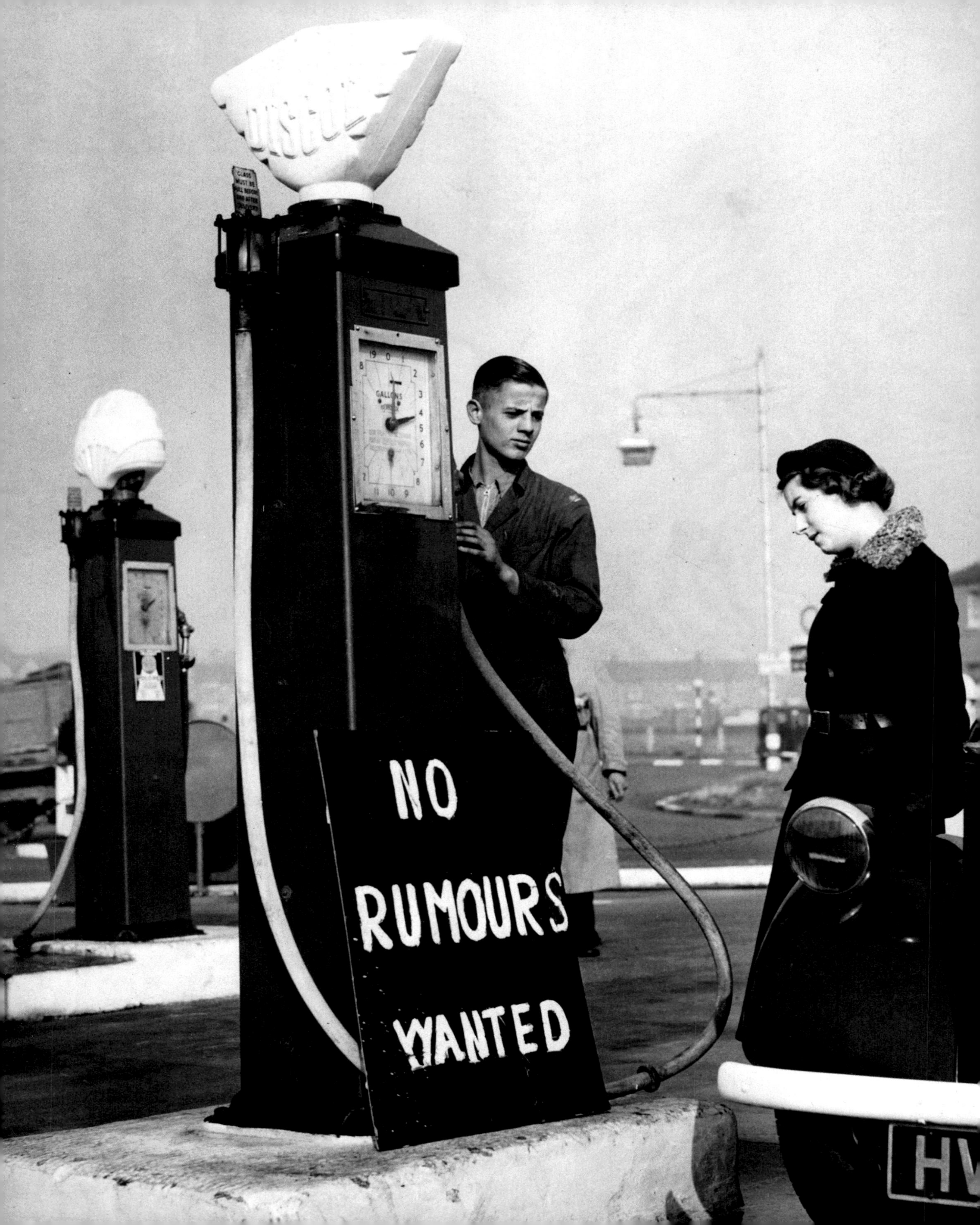
NO
RUMOURS
WANTED

The Gas Station Is Born

The Rhynern rest stop to the south of Hamm on Highway 2 in Germany still stands to this day. The highway was built in the 1930s and was one of the first in Germany. It connects Berlin in the east with the Ruhr region in the west and is one of the country's busiest routes.

anyone in Europe vacationed by the Mediterranean or went skiing in the Alps. Even gas stations embraced the optimistic mood. While prewar gas stations were often only a few pumps placed outside a workshop, their postwar incarnations were very impressive indeed. They might be pushing 70 years old, but the glass, concrete, and steel constructions featuring a pavilion and a canopy are still looking good. \

Gas stations sprang up in previously inaccessible places—the Dolomites, the Alps, and the Pyrenees—their curvaceous, streamlined forms epitomizing the glamour of the Continental tour.

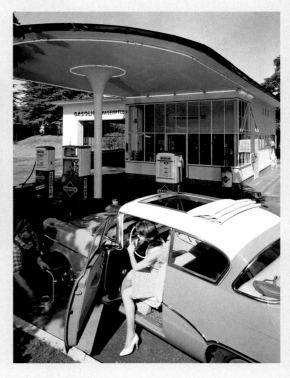

This Shell gas station in Italy was photographed in the early 1960s. Set against the thick fog, it looks like it could be standing at the end of the world. Since rainy weather is actually rare here, the gas pumps are not covered over.

The European New Wave

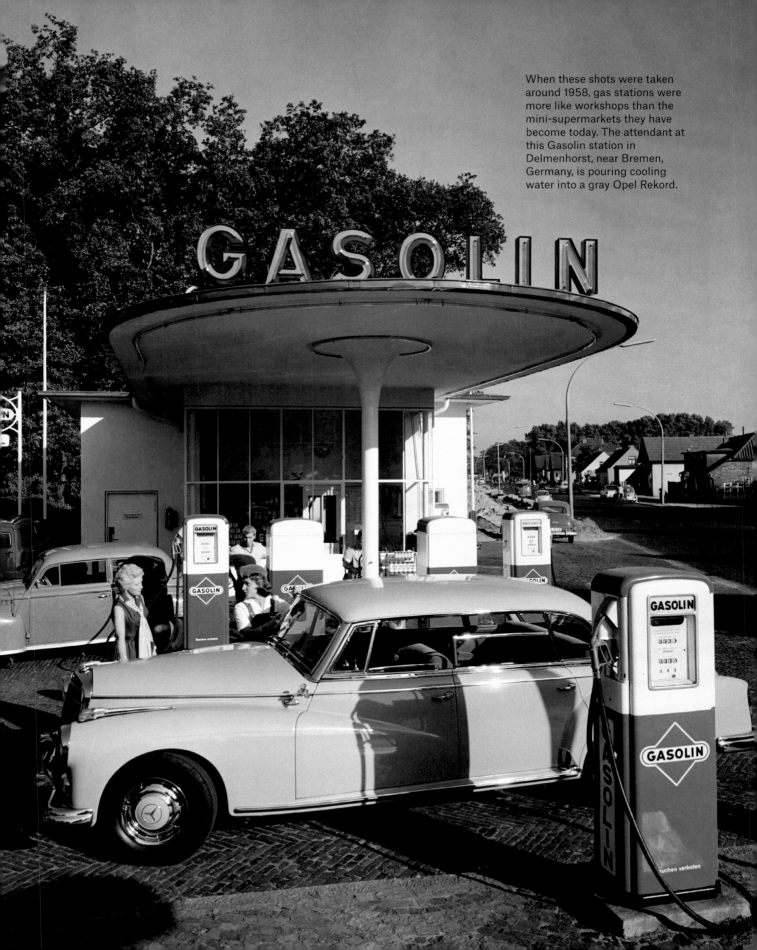

When these shots were taken around 1958, gas stations were more like workshops than the mini-supermarkets they have become today. The attendant at this Gasolin station in Delmenhorst, near Bremen, Germany, is pouring cooling water into a gray Opel Rekord.

With just two pumps and the smallest
of service-station kiosks, this may
not look impressive, but would have
been a welcome sight in the early
years of continental travel, when
opportunities for filling up were few
and far between in such isolated spots.

The European New Wave

Swiss structural engineer Heinz Isler developed thin-walled shells made of reinforced concrete that were inspired by nature rather than any mathematical formula. His designs were used for tennis halls, swimming pools, and this gas station in Deitingen, Switzerland.

This glazed Shell gas station with red garden chairs and umbrellas outside marks a border crossing between Germany and Austria. The picture, taken in 1951, shows a woman quickly checking her tire pressure before heading over the border.

Photographer Isabella Ståhl is famous for nature and landscape shots of her native Sweden: rolling hills, misty forests...and this vintage Esso gas station trying its best to blend in with the wintry white Swedish countryside.

COLOGNE GAS STATIONS

Cologne/Germany

This photo taken by Cologne photographer Carl Detzel in 1956 shows a typical mid-century German gas station at Clevischer Ring in the Mülheim district of his hometown. Gas stations built in Germany in the 1950s and 1960s had a timeless architectural quality to them. With their huge glass windows and flying roofs, the buildings still look modern today, some 60 years later. Instead of displaying company logos, the stations beckoned drivers with a large, simple "T" in a circle—the symbol once used for highway gas stations in Germany. \

SKOVSHOVED GAS STATION BY ARNE JACOBSEN

Copenhagen/Denmark

Gas stations rarely ascend to the ranks of national places of interest. Arne Jacobsen's sleek, white-tiled gas station, built on the outskirts of Copenhagen in 1936, is one of those rare cases. Jacobsen, who is primarily known for his pioneering furniture designs, was contracted in the 1930s to design a new gas station for Texaco. The plan was to build a prototype that would serve as the model for other stations throughout the country. The second part of the plan was never realized, so to see Jacobsen's iconic design, you will have to head to Copenhagen. \

The European New Wave

GOLDEN AGE of the AMERICAN GAS STATION

Everything is bigger in the United States, not least its landscape. With interstate travel on the rise, gas stations became enterprises spawning motels, restaurants, and bars.

Golden Age of the American Gas Station

The sale of gasoline was a lucrative business in the U.S. and companies sought new ways to lure customers. Impressive logos, glamorous forecourts, and an extensive range of services were all the rage.

Gas stations can represent many things: new beginnings, freedom, childhood... And in the U.S. they also symbolize America's economic rise to power. After all, the history of the United States has always been closely linked to the history of oil. American gas stations had their heyday in the 1950s and 1960s, an era when Peter Fonda and Dennis Hopper cruised across the American West on customized Harleys in *Easy Rider*.

Gilmore Gas, with its Red Lion logo, was owned by a farmer lucky enough to strike oil on his land. One of the most successful oil companies of its time, it was unique in marketing gas by its color—red or blue-green.

The movie has retained its cult status to this day. It is one reason why tourists still embark on road trips along Route 66 every year, chasing freedom on the historic highway. The route is lined with gas stations, diners, and motels—some crumbling, some newly restored. Either the country's glory days are long gone or, with a little patience and a whole lot of effort, they are dawning again...it just depends on your lens. \

The wealth generated by rising car ownership was seen in the size of the gas stations that were being built and in the commissioning of leading architects, such as Smith and Williams (top), to design them.

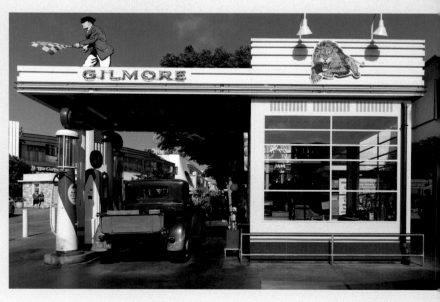

In 1951, the Muller brothers of Los Angeles celebrated their three-millionth car wash with a rather unusual beauty contest. Photographer Allan Grant from *Life* magazine recorded the strange event for posterity. The bathing-suit-clad women were specifically cast for the job and given signs

bearing titles advertising the Muller brothers' wide range of services. There was, for instance, a Miss Body and Fender, a Miss Infra-Red Paint-Job, and a Miss Polish Job. Later versions of this marketing saw women actually washing the cars. Thankfully, that idea did not occur to the Muller brothers. \

In a country where good service is paramount, L.A.'s Muller brothers aimed high. All of their staff wore the same liveried outfits—immaculate white overalls and a chauffeur's cap. The branding smacked of cleanliness and efficiency.

This gas station—called, promisingly, Diamond Service Station—was built in Macon in the U.S. state of Georgia. It was designed by architect Thomas Little; architectural photographer Pedro E. Guerrero captured it in this shot from 1960. The Chevrolet Impala's fins complement the overall design rather well.

David Freund's photographs lend a certain poetry to daily life at American gas stations. The man with the hat and child is clearly headed somewhere, but where? His car is nowhere to be seen.

Route 66 is lined with run-down gas stations that give drivers an idea of what this most historic of roads must have once looked like. This Chevron gas station in Valentine, Mohave County, Arizona, was one of them before it was restored.

For generations of children growing up in small-town America, gas stations were popular places to hang out with friends. They were also a symbol of freedom and wanderlust—after all, the only way to escape the sticks was with a set of wheels and a full tank of gas.

Golden Age of the American Gas Station

Artist and curator David Campany collected 35 press archive images of gas stations taken between 1944 and 1995 for his project Gasoline. Marked with the grease pen notations of newspapers' art directors, the photos tell of oil shortages, road congestion, crimes, accidents and choking cities. Press photos from the collection of David Campany, as featured in his book Gasoline (MACK 2013).

TEXACO

STANDARD

ONE WAY ←

TODAY IN WEST GERMANY GASOLINE 1.35 PER GALLON

In 1978, photographer David Freund received a National Endowment for the Arts grant to travel across the United States and photograph gas stations. The results are snapshots of everyday American life—like this picture of a man working on a 1977 Ford Maverick.

Seligman Sundries is a Route 66
institution in central Arizona.
The building dates back to 1904,
making it one of the oldest in the
small community of Seligman.
It houses a café and a small store
complete with an old-school
vending machine for drinks.

Golden Age of the American Gas Station   79

The 1960s encompassed a decade of enormous upheaval and change. But while young people were growing their hair long and wearing surplus army jackets, car mechanics all over the country were turning up to work clean-shaven—and even wearing shirts and ties under their overalls.

The oil crisis of the 1970s caused gasoline prices to skyrocket and meant that some areas had no gas at all. Cheap offers at a few fuel pumps led drivers to not only fill their tanks, but also their canisters in order to keep their cars running for a few more days.

Golden Age of the American Gas Station

TICHNOR BROTHERS POSTCARD COLLECTION

Boston, MA/United States

In the days when driving was still an adventure, and gas stations were about more than just buying fuel and snacks, it was common to find picture postcards on display in their stores. In the 1930s and 1940s, color photography was still in its infancy, so American motorists waiting for their cars to be fixed would often use the colorful postcards to send greetings to friends and family far away. The Boston Public Library has a collection of these Gatsby-esque postcards, gathered from many different states across the country. \

AILEY'S SERVICE STATION
Route 4 at Main, Fairborn, Ohio

A. R. Arp Esso Service, Benton, Tenn.

76462

83359

P. & L. SERVICE STATION
Pan Am Products — Poplar and Lambuth
Jackson, Tenn.

77143

Western Service Station Inc., Wendover, Utah

Orange Auto Service, Orange, Texas

80294

Across the street from Keown Supply Co.

80294

BRADFORD FILLING STATION
Main at Congress
Bradford, Pa.

Roberts Texaco Service
623 Holcombe Ave.
Phone 6-9282   Mobile, Ala.

8 1165

67081

Hermes Central Station
John D. Hermes
Bradford, Pa.

81803

Twin Gables

Hermes Kendall Station
John D. Hermes
Custer City, Pa.

67082

Joe Hartnett's Atlantic Station, 5th and Somerville Ave., Phila, Pa.

78749

"TRY US" for service, see the difference".

78749

REPINE'S
KENDALL SERVICE STATION
Cor. Chase and Field Sts.
Kane, Pa.

82054

HEISHMAN'S SUNOCO SERVICE AND RESTAURANT
HARRISBURG PIKE AT NEW KINGSTON, PENNA.

Photographer George Marks captured this Gulf station in the U.S. in the early 1950s. It combines a streamlined modern style with art deco elements. The result is a pairing of long, horizontal lines and curved corners and forms.

This "skewered" gas station sits at the foot of the Grand Canyon. Two slender needles are all that support the heavy roof. The laundromat next door is called Radiator Springs; in the Pixar animation *Cars,* the fictional town of the same name is situated on Route 66.

A father and daughter stand by the family's four-wheeled pride and joy: a 1947 Mercury Club Coupe convertible. The father's rockabilly look—checked shirt, sturdy jeans, and leather boots—has hardly changed at all in the past 70 years.

John Margolies photographed this branch of the 76 gas station chain in Tucson, Arizona, in 1979. The name "76" refers to the United States Declaration of Independence of 1776 and to the octane number of the gasoline that the company introduced in 1932.

Roy's is situated in a tiny town in San Bernardino County, on the National Trails Highway of Route 66 within California's Mojave Desert. The futuristic gas station, along with its motel and café, are considered prime examples of 1950s Googie architecture.

MOBIL GAS STATION

Anaheim, CA/United States

No photographer is associated more closely with American post-war modernist architecture than Julius Shulman. With their clear visual language, his shots of buildings by the likes of Richard Neutra and Pierre Koenig established architectural photography as an art form in its own right. In 1956, Shulman photographed this gas station that his friends Whitney Smith and Wayne Williams had designed for Mobil in Anaheim, California, close to Disneyland. Shulman composed the photos spontaneously. The red car belonged to a customer, and the white gloves belonged to the wife of one of the architects. \

FROM *SIBERIA* to MYANMAR

From the modest roadside shack to the gilt-edged oil emporium, one look at a gas station can reveal all there is to know about a country's economic and cultural identity.

From Siberia to Myanmar

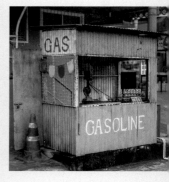

Wherever you are in the world, you will find people filling up on gas—under garish neon signs in Japan, outside a corrugated-iron shack in Kiev, from a glass bottle by the roadside in Indonesia, or out of a simple gas pump. Gas stations are among the most widespread and easily recognizable types of building. Restaurants and places of worship might look different from one region to the next, but you can usually spot a gas station. That said, a

Sometimes improvisation is necessary—and more economical. This gas station in Sapoljarnoje, western Siberia, is simply tapping into a natural gas field.

There are many places in the world where the money simply isn't there to replace outmoded gas stations on a regular basis; catching sight of such places can sometimes feel like stepping back in time.

gas station is also a reflection of local identity, an architectural expression of the way a place sees itself. Lonely gas pumps in the middle of nowhere in Iceland are the picture of peace and solitude. To get a good idea of Texan identity, look at a Buc-ee's gas station in New Braunfels, with its 60 gas pumps, 1,000 parking spaces, 250 employees, and 80 soda machines. The store alone is 6,300 square meters—roughly the size of a soccer field. \

In some parts of the world, gas is still sold by the liter in bottles to save the expense of a pump and all that goes with it. At this gas station in Thailand, vehicle owners can buy gas stored in recycled spirit bottles.

The gas pump is probably the most characteristic element of the gas station. Collectors are willing to pay several thousands for well-preserved pumps from decades past. Today, they are a popular addition to the decor in workshops, bars, and even people's homes. The first gas pumps were installed in the

1920s. They had a large crank that was used to pump the gas by hand. The tall, slender, and slightly curved pumps from this period were known affectionately as "iron maidens" in Germany. Pumps became smaller in the 1930s and were outfitted with a gauge so users could see how much gas they had pumped. \

Eugenio Grosso photographed gas
stations on a jouirney from Erbil, the
capital city of Iraqi Kurdistan, to
Sulaymaniyah, the second largest city
in the region. Stretching for a good
100 kilometers, the road presented
Grosso with numerous gas stations
that were remarkably varied in terms
of their design and features.

From Siberia to Myanmar

From Siberia to Myanmar

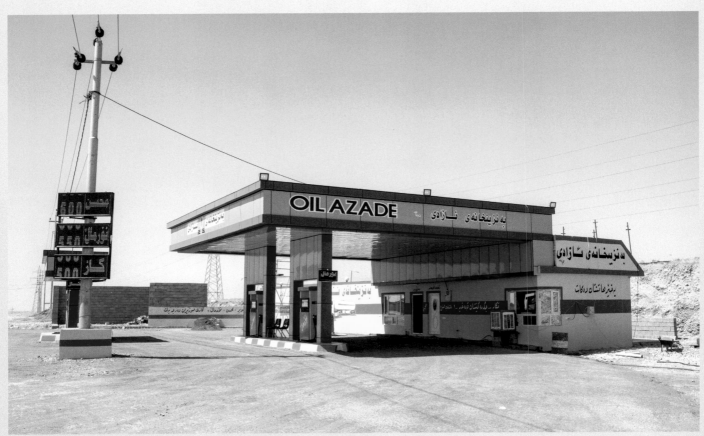

From Siberia to Myanmar

If you were to take the expression "black gold" literally, you might end up with a gas station that looks a bit like this. The incredibly opulent edifice in Iraq is all the more striking when compared to nearby gas stations, most of which comprise a few pumps and a shipping container.

CEPSA SERVICE STATION

Adanero / Spain

The Spanish energy company Cepsa commissioned Saffron, a consultancy firm, with designing a new brand image. The consultants describe the essence of Cepsa as highly technological yet very customer-focused. To resolve this apparent contradiction, they developed the concept of "adaptable engineering." The idea was for Cepsa's gas stations (the brand's contact point) to communicate the duality to the public. Working with designers from Tangerine and Malka&Portús, Saffron created a gas station that expresses the company's values via modern materials and forms and a friendly, customer-oriented ambiance. \

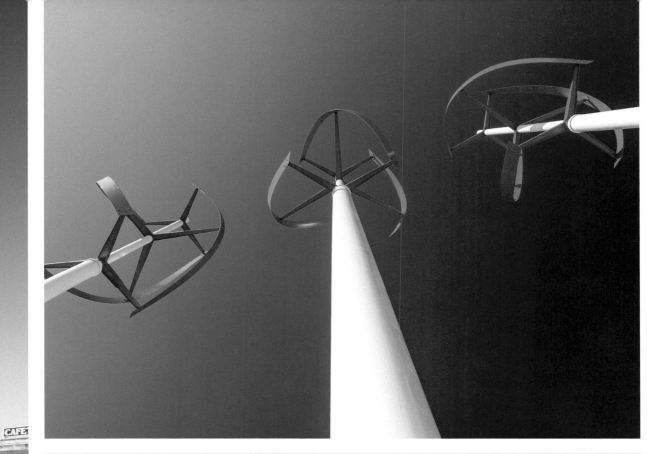

From Siberia to Myanmar

安全 ✚ 第 一

Noé Baruchel Dominati discovered this Greek gas station on the Ionian Sea. The island of Lefkada has a steep coastline with buildings arranged in steps. The gas station looks like a fleeting construction on the edge of the port, and attracts customers with its "water-free" promise.

Multiple skyscrapers—not least the world's tallest, the Burj Khalifa—dominate the skyline above an *ENOC* gas station. Although Dubai is now taking steps to diversify its economy in preparation for when oil reserves run dry, the growth of this city still owes much to proceeds from the sale of petroleum and natural gas.

From Siberia to Myanmar

No place is too remote for filling up these days. This gas station is on the Socotra Island, which lies some 185 miles off the coast of Yemen in the Gulf of Aden. Concrete umbrellas shield patrons from the heat of the sun as they fill their vehicles.

This gas station is located on the Yangon-Mandalay Expressway, which connects Myanmar's former capital Yangon (Rangoon) with the city of Mandalay. The fanciful pink-and-yellow building looks like a millipede made of bubble gum.

While traveling through Myanmar, photographer Craig Easton found himself on the road to Mandalay (made famous by Frank Sinatra and Robbie Williams). He noticed how unique the gas stations were, and so—just like Ed Ruscha—he photographed 26 of them.

From Siberia to Myanmar

Roadside *NOVELTY:* ANYTHING GOES

Knowing that they can never compete with the lower prices of the giant oil companies, smaller enterprises have learned to take a novel approach to getting noticed.

Roadside Novelty: Anything Goes

With the speed at which drivers are whizzing by, gas station operators need to think like entrepreneurs and fight loudly to stay in business. Most gas stations try to grab people's attention with garish colors and neon signs, while some try to achieve the same effect with more attractive designs. And then there is a whole series of stations that stand out because they look... well... different. So different, in fact, that you might have to look twice. Think gas stations shaped like a teapot, a cowboy hat, or accompanied

by a religious scene. "Experience marketing" is a term economists use to describe buying that becomes an experience the customer can still remember weeks later. Gas stations do not have a whole lot of leeway for this—at least in terms of the products—and a driver's decision to buy gas from Shell or Total depends mainly on the price, not on brand loyalty. So when making that pit stop for gas, a memorable space might just go the extra mile. \

In 2008, the International Fiber Collaborative launched a project that sought to wrap abandoned gas stations in creative panels. Other artists and enthusiasts continue to feature gas station paraphernalia as part of their work.

There is always room for a little gimmickry at the gas station—whatever it takes to lure a new customer. From roller skates to toy models of the enterprise or outlets shaped as tepees, the forecourt has seen it all.

In 1947, this Second World War B-17 bomber was flown to Milwaukie, Oregon, where it served as a canopy for this gas station until 1991. It was later adopted by the Bomber Restaurant before being dismantled in 2014.

The "oriental" style of this gas station in West Allis, Wisconsin, was the work of architect Alexander Eschweiler, who was commissioned to design something striking for Wadhams Oil & Grease Company in 1916. This iconic example was built in 1927 and restored in 2000.

Constructed in 1936, the world's largest Redwood Tree Service Station can be found in Ukiah, California and features the stump of a 1,500-year-old tree measuring 81 feet in circumference. Today, visitors can take themselves on a tour of the interior, which now serves as a museum.

Tepees, the traditional tents used by Native Americans, were a popular symbol of the dream to travel—as shown by this gas station in Kansas, part of a motel chain whose slogan asks, "Have you slept in a wigwam lately?"

Roadside Novelty: Anything Goes

This photo of the *Save Way Gas Station* in Texas was taken by architectural critic and curator John Margolies, who spent four decades recording vernacular commercial architecture on America's highways and byways. *The John Margolies Roadside America Photograph Archive* totals more than eleven thousand images.

ESSO GAS STATION

The Hague/The Netherlands

Dutch architect Willem Marinus Dudok designed a simple Esso gas station in the early 1950s, with 112 more built along Dutch highways. This replica (opposite, bottom right) has been on display in The Hague since 2004—but if you have the right Lego blocks, you can build your own replica at home. \

The Teapot Dome scandal was the
biggest political bribery scandal of
1920s America, and it remained a
symbol of corruption for decades
afterward. This gas station was built in
1922 in Yakima County, Washington,
as a reminder of the crime.

Roadside Novelty: Anything Goes

165

Hat 'n' Boots was originally part of the Premium Tex gas station, which was built in 1954 just south of Seattle. The boots housed bathrooms, and the fire-engine-red hat sat atop a small store. The gas station closed in 1988, but the hat and boots are still standing.

REST ROOMS

Fire Chief

Fire Chief

Roadside Novelty: Anything Goes

At first sight, this Chevron station in Vancouver, British Columbia, might look a bit odd. But once you realize that motorboats need gasoline too, this image of a floating gas station makes a whole lot more sense.

Irish artist Maser transformed an abandoned gas station in the southwest of Ireland into a surreal installation. The title, *No. 27—A Nod to Ed Ruscha,* is a tongue-in-cheek reference to 26 photographic works from the famous artist on the same subject.

Graphic designer duo Craig&Karl
(a.k.a. Craig Redman and Karl Maier)
are probably best known for their
vibrant pop-art magazine covers.
They transformed this abandoned gas
station in London's White City into
a flamboyantly patterned event space.

Roadside Novelty: Anything Goes

RE-DISCOVERING the GAS STATION

The gas station has always posed an architectural challenge as designers seek to add character while meeting the station's functional needs.

Rediscovering the Gas Station

Belgian architects Samyn and Partners opted for a neon-lit, glazed steel structure and raked awnings for shelter. Their twenty-first-century approach mirrors that of Mies van der Rohe's 1960s design in Quebec, Canada (top of opposite page).

Although gas stations are functionally simple buildings, they can pose an architectural challenge. They require easy accessibility for driving up to the pump, but should ideally be attractive too, encouraging drivers to slow down, stop, and linger a while. Many oil companies opt for the standard design: flat, garishly lit canopies with attention-grabbing price

Quirky cantilevers are a mainstay of gas station architecture, and German photographer Tim Hölscher has revamped existing buildings digitally in order to showcase the structural elements that make them unique.

signs. However, a new generation of architects are trying to reinvent the gas station and, as a series of radical new designs shows, they are succeeding. While Atelier SAD placed giant umbrella-like canopies on the roadside in Slovakia, Samyn and Partners drew inspiration from tents, and Elliott + Associates built a monument to soda. \

Taking a brutalist approach, Czech firm Atelier SAD favors the mainstay of modern architecture—reinforced concrete—to create elegant, curvaceous shelters raised on a series of vertical columns.

This gas station looks more than a little like the Neue Nationalgalerie in Berlin—and for good reason. Architect Ludwig Mies van der Rohe is responsible for both buildings with their clean lines, narrow steel pillars, and seemingly floating roofs. Situated in Montreal, the station was turned into a community center in 2002.

Acciona, a renewable fuels supplier, asked the architects at AH Asociados to design an unconventional gas station that embodies the company's values. The result is this building, which is located between Pamplona and Logroño, Spain, and features an eye-catching jagged wooden roof.

The architects at Samyn and Partners describe their tent-like design as a "dramatic departure from traditional gas stations with their single steel canopy." Also absent? The typical neon writing and garish friezes.

This wave-like gas station canopy follows the undulations of the hills close to San Agustín del Guadalix, north of Madrid. Moneo Brock, the architecture firm behind the project, created a canopy that blended respectfully into its environment.

The architects at Samyn and Partners have created a whole series of gas stations that break with the usual industry-standard design. This station, built for the French oil company Total in Minderhout, Belgium, is perhaps one of their most traditional designs.

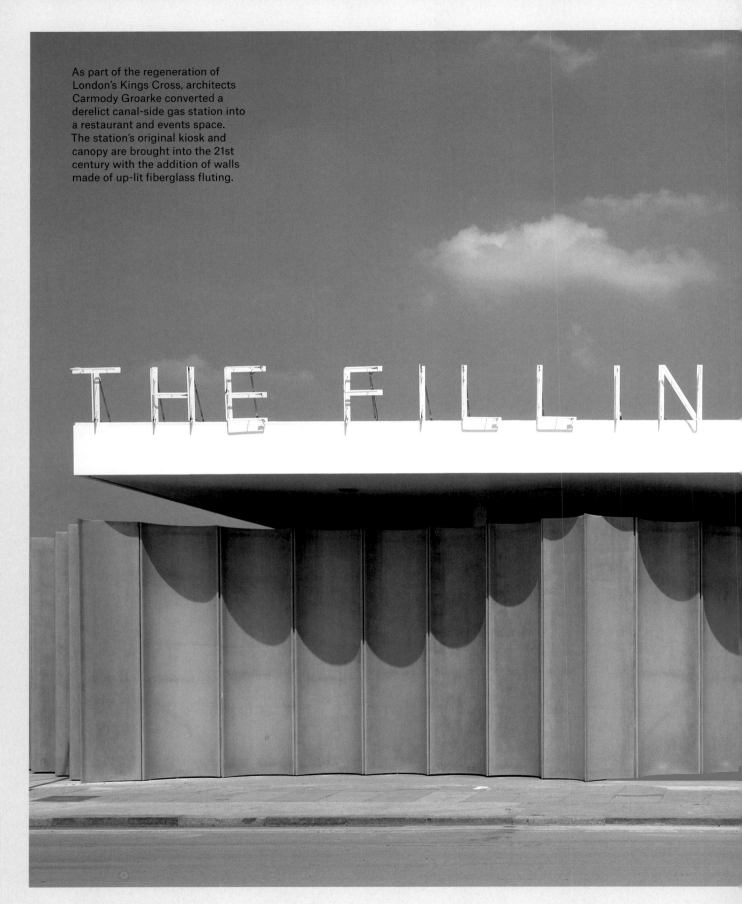

As part of the regeneration of London's Kings Cross, architects Carmody Groarke converted a derelict canal-side gas station into a restaurant and events space. The station's original kiosk and canopy are brought into the 21st century with the addition of walls made of up-lit fiberglass fluting.

THE FILLIN

a little better

000925

Los Angeles *Helios House* gas station was built in 2007 in a bid to create a model for the future. A major feature is the station's roof, which is made from recycled stainless steel and contains cacti and solar panels. It is drought tolerant and collects water for irrigation.

GAS STATION AND MCDONALD'S

Batumi / Georgia

McDonald's restaurants are not immediately associated with modern architecture. Their distinctive mansard roofs, first introduced in the late 1960s and then redesigned several times over the years, might be iconic—but modern? This branch, housed in a glass gas station in Batumi, Georgia's second-largest city, bucks that trend. The building was completed in 2013 and designed by the architectural firm Giorgi Khmaladze. The gas station is hidden behind the modern geometric structure's glass façade, allowing it to blend seamlessly into the city center's surroundings. \

Rediscovering the Gas Station

Photographer Stefan Oláh wants his pictures to capture the Vienna that he has grown to love. When he realized that the city's gas stations were disappearing, he set about documenting the most interesting of the remaining structures—like this Shell gas station on Hadikgasse.

Rediscovering the Gas Station 197

For his Tankstelle project, German photographer Tim Hölscher wanted to focus purely on gas station architecture. After photographing old gas stations, he digitally returned them to their original condition and cut them out of their usual surroundings.

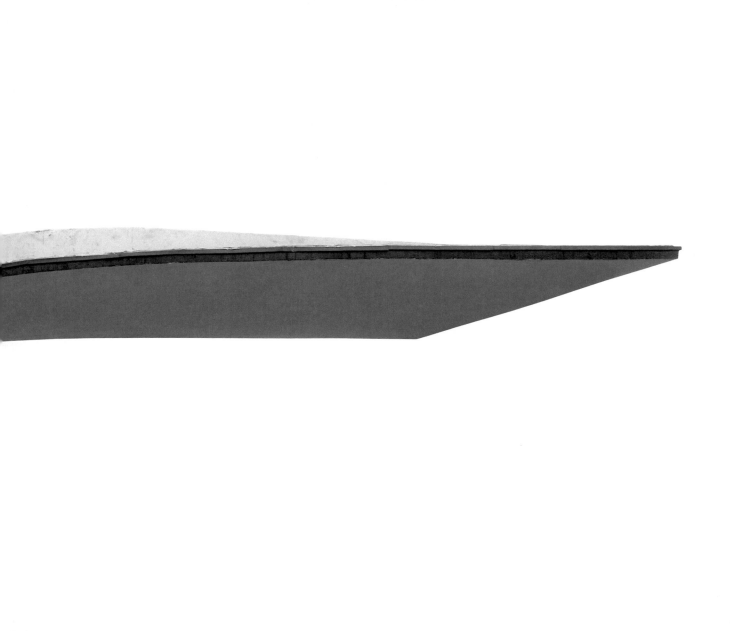

GAS STATION MATÚŠKOVO

Matúškovo/Slovakia

Three concrete pillars support three concrete discs that appear to melt into each other. Rings of light circle the areas where the pillars and discs meet, making the gas station look like a heavy concrete UFO coming in for landing. The building, which was completed in 2011, is located in Slovakia, about 25 kilometers east of the capital Bratislava. It is based on a design by the architects at Atelier SAD. Reduced to its essential elements, the gas station was no more expensive to build than conventional versions, but it manages to present and cultivate its components in a new style. \

Rediscovering the Gas Station

Rediscovering the Gas Station

REST STOP GORI

Gori/Georgia

In 2009, Berlin architecture firm J. Mayer H. was commissioned to design 20 highway rest stops for a new transit route in Georgia that would connect Azerbaijan with Turkey. The rest stops are situated at scenic locations along the highway and house more than just the usual filling stations and supermarkets. With exhibition spaces, assembly rooms, and small farmers' markets selling local produce, the buildings double as meeting places for local residents and those just passing through. The design, which was led by Paul Angelier, won the Architizer A+Award in 2013. \

REST STOP LOCHINI

Lochini/Georgia

While the building on the preceding pages features brutalist elements and sharp edges, this design is more restrained and organic. Depending on your viewing angle, the white gas station with its curved lines might look like a cloud, a microbe, or something entirely different. It does not, however, look like a normal gas station, which is why drivers probably have to look twice before they realize that they can fill up on gas here. \

POPS GAS STATION

Arcadia, OK/United States

The gas stations and diners that alternate along Route 66 are as legendary as the road itself. The architecture firm Elliott + Associates was tasked with reinterpreting this package and designing a rest area that is both functional and inviting. The result is Pops, Arcadia, situated just outside of Oklahoma City. TV network CNBC called it "the coolest gas station you've ever seen." Motorists are greeted by a giant soda bottle that is visible for miles around. The interior is all about taste: with 486 different kinds of soda on offer, Pops is as much about selling variety as it is about selling a sense of freedom. \

Rediscovering the Gas Station

TOTALFINA SERVICE STATION AND RESTAURANT

Hellebecq/Belgium

The architects at Samyn and Partners in Brussels designed this gas station for Total. It is located in rural Belgium, close to Hellebecq. Designed to look like a flourishing garden, the station aims to bring travelers into contact with nature and the regional culture. The sheet-metal roof is styled after Belgian greenhouses and supported by narrow columns. Viewed from a distance, it looks as if the roof is hovering in mid-air. The dining area is situated in a beamless bridge that spans the highway—making it the perfect pit stop for enjoying expansive views across the Belgian countryside. \

FINA EUROPE SERVICE STATION

Houten/The Netherlands

When the oil corporation Petrofina decided it wanted something different from the usual gas station, it asked the architects at Samyn and Partners to come up with an unorthodox design for a project in Houten, the Netherlands. While conventional gas stations usually carry a flat roof, this one has a slightly slanted one designed to be inviting to travelers. In addition, the architects enclosed the site with a steel fence. It acts as a windbreaker, but also makes visitors feel secure while right next to the highway. \

GHOST TOWN GAS STATIONS

There is little that beats the romance of abandoned gas stations. Once lively pit stops for road-trippers, their fall from grace came as the golden age of flying was ushered in.

Ghost Town Gas Stations

Gas stations in remote places are simply left to fester—they are expensive to dismantle. In comes faded, peeling paintwork; dry, cracked forecourts; crumbling façades; and broken neon signage.

Photographing abandoned buildings has become extremely popular around the world in the last decade. Capturing and displaying transience is particularly fascinating when a place tells a story of societal change. In the case of gas stations, we now have an entire industry that must keep up with technological innovations such as e-mobility. Abandoned gas stations have a charm all of their own. Perhaps this is because they were built alongside roads (such as the iconic Route 66), putting their gradual decay on

display as one drives past. Or perhaps it is because gas stations were once more varied in their aesthetic. The market is dominated by a few large chains today, whereas it was divided between numerous small businesses throughout the twentieth century. This also meant that the architecture was more diverse. Examining abandoned gas stations gives us a glimpse into the past, one where cars meant more than status. They also represented freedom, with gas stations the springboards into the wild blue yonder. \

With just a few remnants remaining, the abandoned gas station adopts an air of incongruity. Anyone passing through would be right to grab a camera—and question how such a place could have been busy in the first place.

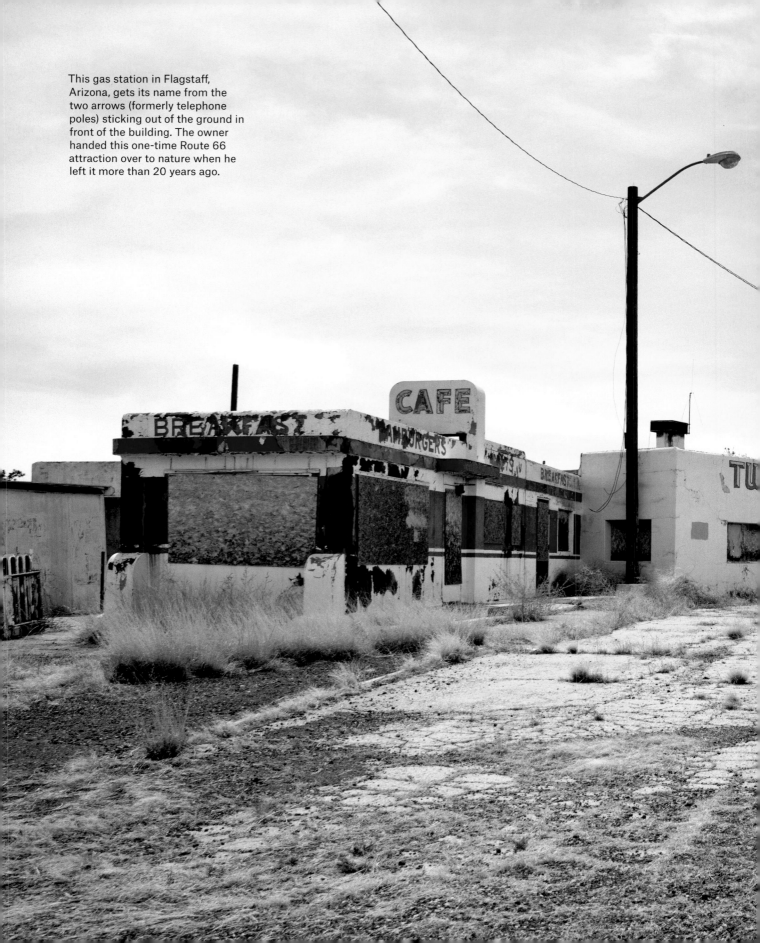

This gas station in Flagstaff, Arizona, gets its name from the two arrows (formerly telephone poles) sticking out of the ground in front of the building. The owner handed this one-time Route 66 attraction over to nature when he left it more than 20 years ago.

The Mohawk people, who call themselves People of the Flint, are a Native American tribe from the region east of Lake Ontario. The Mohawk Mini-Mart and its gas station are located on Route 66 in Oro Grande in California's Mojave Desert.

The Road Runner's Retreat was a restaurant and gas station on historic Route 66 in the heart of the Californian desert, just 15 kilometers east of the iconic Roy's Motel and Café. The staff used to live in small trailers behind the restaurant.

With diffused light and set against an overcast sky, this abandoned Russian Lukoil gas station, near to the border with Kazakhstan, looks almost like the backdrop to a dystopian sci-fi film.

These lampposts rise up like giraffe necks in Nevada's Great Basin, close to the Utah border. The gas station itself has been disused for a long time—presumably too remote to turn a profit.

Contrary to what its name implies, this gas station, photographed by John Margolies in 1986, is located in Detroit, Michigan, 1,500 kilometers from Oklahoma. You'll find it on Livernois Avenue, a major thoroughfare in the west of the city.

If this was a gas and service station, it wouldn't exactly be convenient, with no roads for miles around. In truth, this is a Swedish barn designed to look like a retro Gulf station, complete with authentic signage—a great find for any location scout.

Lush greenery, blue skies, vintage gas pumps, and a rustic shed make this trailer park in the U.S. state of Virginia look more romantic than it might be. The vintage Chevy Malibu (the first generation of which was built between 1964 and 1972) adds to the appeal.

INDEX

OFFICE DA AND JOHNSTON MARKLEE

johnstonmarklee.com
United States
Helios House
Los Angeles, California, United States
Photo credit: Getty images/Carlos Chavez
Pages: 192–193

PANORAMIC IMAGES

panoramicimages.com
Photo credit: Thomas Winz/Panoramic Images
Pages: 168–169

RICK PISIO

rwphotos.com
United States
Gas Stations
Western United States
Pages: 220 (tl, tr), 222–223

ROBERT GOETZFRIED

robert-goetzfried.com
Germany
Fill 'er up
Virginia, United States
Pages: 236–237

ROLAND ROSSNER

roland-rossner.de
Germany
Rhynern Rest Stop
Rhynern, Germany
Pages: 28–29

SAFFRON

saffron-consultants.com
Spain
Cepsa Service Station
Adanero, Spain
Photo credit: Montse Zamorano/montsezamorano.com
Pages: 128–131

SAMYN AND PARTNERS

samynandpartners.be
Belgium

515–2 Total Belgium S.A. – Service Stations - Aire De Ruisbroeck
Ruisbroeck, Belgium
Photo credit: Quentin Olbrechts
Page: 178 (tl)

435 Totalfinaelf Belgium s.a. – Service Station in Minderhout
Minderhout, Belgium
Photo credit: Marie-Françoise Plissart
Pages: 188–189

386-Totalfina Belgium – Service Stations and Restaurant
Hellebecq, Belgium
Photo credit: Marie-Françoise Plissart
Pages: 214–215

363-Fina Europe: Service Station – Houten
Houten, Netherlands
Photo credit: Christian Richters
Pages: 216–217

314-Fina Europe: Petrol Stations Highway E411
Wanlin, Belgium
Photo credit: Serge Brison
Pages: 184–185

SMITH AND WILLIAMS

United States
Mobil Gas Station
Anaheim, California, United States
Photo credit: © J. Paul Getty Trust. Getty Research Institute, Los Angeles (2004.R.10)
Pages: 61 (t), 108–111

STEFAN OLÁH

olah.at
Austria
Sechsundzwanzig Wiener Tankstellen
Vienna, Austria
Pages: 115 (tl), 116, 196–197

THOMAS LITTLE

United States
Diamond Service Station
Macon, Georgia, United States
Photo credit: The Estate of Pedro E. Guerrero, Courtesy of Edward Cella Art & Architecture
Pages: 58–59, 64–65

TIM HÖLSCHER

timhoelscher.de
Germany

Zapfsäulen
Pages: 116–117

Gas Stations
Pages: 178 (tr, bl), 179 (bl, br), 198–201

WILLEM MARINUS DUDOK

The Netherlands
Esso Gas Station
Photo credit: Andrea Lattanzio
Page: 160–163

IMAGE CREDITS

AKG-IMAGES

Photo credit: akg-images, Page: 34

Photo credit: akg-images/Elizaveta Becker, Page: 114 (br)

Photo credit: akg-images, Page: 8

Photo credit: akg-images, Page: 27

Photo credit: akg-images, Page: 23

Photo credit: akg-images, Page: 9, 116

Photo credit: akg-images, Page: 2, 20

Photo credit: akg-images, Page: 6 (bl)

Photo credit: akg-images/Dodenhoff, Page: 32 (tr)

Photo credit: akg-images/Dodenhoff, Page: 33 (br)

Photo credit: akg-images/Dodenhoff, Page: 38

Photo credit: akg-images/Dodenhoff, Page: 39

Photo credit: akg-images, Page: 7, 22

Photo credit: akg-images/Paul Almasy, Page: 14

Photo credit: akg-images/Paul Almasy, Page: 149 (t)

Photo credit: akg-images, Page: 16

Photo credit: akg-images, Pages: 6 (br), 117

Photo credit: akg-images/Paul Almasy, Page: 116

ALAMY

Photo credit: imageBROKER/Alamy Stock Foto, Page: 114 (br)

Photo credit: imageBROKER/Alamy Stock Foto, Page: 117

Photo credit: ADS/Alamy Stock Photo, Page: 117

Photo credit: Oriol Alamany/Alamy Stock Photo, Page: 138

Photo credit: Elena Odareeva/Alamy Stock Photo, Page: 117

Photo credit: Frank Bienewald/Alamy Stock Photo, Page: 116

Photo credit: Piotr Stryjewski/Alamy Stock Foto, Page: 114 (tr)

Photo credit: Alamy Stock Foto, Page: 157

ALINARI

Photo credit: UIG/Archivi Alinari, Page: 33 (bl)

Photo credit: Archivi Alinari, Firenze, Page: 116

Photo credit: Archivi Alinari, Firenze, Page: 40

Photo credit: Archivi Alinari, Firenze, Page: 36

Photo credit: Archivi Alinari, Firenze, Page: 32 (tl)

BILDARCHIV AUSTRIA

Photo credit: ÖNB/Rübelt, Page: 2 (tr)

Photo credit: ÖNB/Rübelt, Page: 44

Photo credit: ÖNB/Rübelt, Page: 33 (t)

Photo credit: ÖNB/Rübelt, Page: 10

BILDERBUCH KÖLN

Photo credit: Bilderbuch Köln, Pages: 48–51

BUNDESARCHIV

bundesarchiv.de
Photo credit: Bundesarchiv, Bild 183-1989-1109-030 / Photography: Matthias Hiekel, Page: 32 (b)

DEUTSCHE FOTOTHEK

Photo credit: Page: 12

GETTY

Photo credit: Getty images, Page: 61 (bl)

Photo credit: Getty images/sodapix sodapix, Page: 117

Photo credit: Getty images/Mark D Callanan, Page: 148 (tl)

Photo credit: Getty images/The Life Picture Collection/Allan Grant, Pages: 62–63

Photo credit: Getty images/Fox Photos/Stringer, Page: 6 (t)

Photo credit: Getty images/George Marks/Stringer, Page: 97

Photo credit: Getty images/Joe Daniel Price, Page: 170

Photo credit: Getty images/Hulton Deutsch, Pages: 5, 26

Photo credit: Getty images/PBNJ Productions, Page: 100

Photo credit: Getty images/Bill Stormont, Page: 230

Photo credit: Getty images/H. Armstrong Roberts, Page: 80

INTERFOTO

Photo credit: INTERFOTO/TV-Yesterday, Page: 149 (bl)

ISTOCK

Photo credit: iStock/Feifei Cui-Paoluzzo, Page: 76

It's a GAS!

The Allure of the Gas Station

This book was conceived, edited, and designed by Gestalten.

Edited by Robert Klanten and Sally Fuls
Contributing Editor: Sascha Friesike

Preface by Jay Leno
Text by Sascha Friesike
Translation from German to English by Jen Metcalf
Additional text by Anna Southgate (pp. 4–7, 24,
30–33, 40, 52, 58–61, 112–115, 136, 139, 146–149, 152, 155,
159, 176–179, 190, 193, 218–221)

Project Management by Adam Jackman

Design and Layout by Jeannine Moser
Creative Direction of Design by Ludwig Wendt
Cover by Ludwig Wendt

Typefaces: Atlas Grotesk by Christian Schwartz,
Susana Carvalho, and Kai Bernau;
Sign Painter by Ken Barber;
and Kolg Gothic by Greg Ponchak

Cover photography: © J. Paul Getty Trust.
Getty Research Institute, Los Angeles (2004.R.10)
Printed by Printer Trento S.r.l, Trento, Italy
Made in Europe
Published by Gestalten, Berlin 2018
ISBN 978-3-89955-928-6

For more information, and to order books, please visit
www.gestalten.com.

Bibliographic information published by the Deutsche
Nationalbibliothek.
The Deutsche Nationalbibliothek lists this publication in
the Deutsche Nationalbibliografie;
detailed bibliographic data are available online at
http://dnb.d-nb.de.

None of the content in this book was published in exchange
for payment by commercial parties or designers; Gestalten
selected all included work based solely on its artistic merit.

This book was printed on paper certified according to the
standards of the FSC®.

FSC
www.fsc.org
MIX
Paper from
responsible sources
FSC® C015829